UNIVERSITY OF CAMBRIDGE

Classic CAMBRIDGE
University Edition

Classic CAMBRIDGE

CAMBRIDGE ARMS
Coats of Arms of the City,
the University
&
the Colleges

CAMBRIDGE CITY

*c.*500 B.C.

CAMBRIDGE UNIVERSITY

*c.*1209

College	Image	Date
PETERHOUSE		1284
CLARE		1326
PEMBROKE		1347
GONVILLE & CAIUS		1348
TRINITY HALL		1350
CORPUS CHRISTI		1352
KING'S		1441

PETERHOUSE — 1284
CLARE — 1326
PEMBROKE — 1347
GONVILLE & CAIUS — 1348
TRINITY HALL — 1350
CORPUS CHRISTI — 1352
KING'S — 1441

QUEENS' — 1448
ST. CATHARINE'S — 1473
JESUS — 1496
CHRIST'S — 1505
ST. JOHN'S — 1511
MAGDALENE — 1542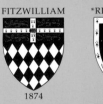
TRINITY — 1546

EMMANUEL — 1584
SIDNEY SUSSEX — 1594
DOWNING — 1800
GIRTON — 1869
NEWNHAM — 1871
FITZWILLIAM — 1874
*RIDLEY HALL — 1877

SELWYN — 1879
*WESTCOTT HOUSE — 1881
HUGHES HALL — 1885
HOMERTON — 1894
ST. EDMUND'S — 1896
*WESLEY HOUSE — 1921
MURRAY EDWARDS — 1954

CHURCHILL — 1958
LUCY CAVENDISH — 1965
DARWIN — 1965
CLARE HALL — 1965
WOLFSON — 1965
ROBINSON — 1977

*Affiliated Theological College *(Note: Christ's and St John's both foundations of Lady Margaret Beaufort)*
The University Coat of Arms is reproduced under licence from the University of Cambridge

For my children, born in Cambridge

Katie, Ed, Jamie & Ellie

Classic CAMBRIDGE

100 Photographs by
TIM RAWLE

Classic CAMBRIDGE

100 Photographs by Tim Rawle

Published by The Cambridge Portfolio Ltd.
www.cambridge-portfolio.co.uk

First published in 2012

ISBN: 978-0-9572867-0-2

British Library Cataloguing in Publication Data
A CIP catalogue record for this book is
available from the British Library.

Designed by Tim Rawle.
Printed and bound in the UK by
Butler Tanner & Dennis Ltd.,
Frome, Somerset.

INTRODUCTION

Cambridge is an exceptional and beautiful city with a centre that has evolved over almost a thousand years into this magical place. Though very English it is also cosmopolitan, with many languages easily overheard around the café and bistro culture that is now part of our urban fabric. In Cambridge this is not only due to the millions of visiting tourists, but also to the rich multi-cultural community in both the university and the city, to the expansion of local industry on an international scale, and to the many language schools based here. As home to one of the top universities in the world, this East Anglian market town has risen to fame far beyond its initial prospects, a journey that has not always been easy.

Throughout history Cambridge has been a regional hub owing to its river crossing, making it of strategic importance from Roman times. In the long and turbulent Dark Ages this corner of England bore the onslaught of Viking invasions while Saxons and Danes fought over it for centuries, the Danes establishing Cambridge as a major inland port, essential to its early development. The momentous Norman Conquest in 1066, under William the Conqueror, then brought relative stability, allowing county towns such as Cambridge to grow and prosper.

In the early years of the 13th century the residents of Cambridge campaigned for the freedom of the borough from the crown, which was successfully achieved in 1207 giving the community more autonomy. Shortly after this the most important 'invasion' in Cambridge's long history took place when a group of scholars fled from Oxford, seeking refuge after riots with the townsfolk, some of these scholars having originally been from the Cambridge area. Although teaching existed in Oxford as early as 1096 and grew rapidly in the 1100's, there is no clear date for the foundation of the university, the earliest verified date being 1201. There had also been a learned community in Cambridge for many years around this time, in the form of friars in their religious houses, and it is thought

that was a major reason why those academic refugees headed to this then remote place in the East Anglian Fens. The arrival of the Oxford scholars in 1209 marks the start of the university in Cambridge. At that time the residents had no idea how the future of their town would be gradually transformed by the establishment of the university and its colleges into the world famous place it is today. Thus we have the beginnings of the two great English universities embarking on their age-old 'Oxbridge' rivalry lasting for centuries to come. No other universities were founded in England for another 600 years.

This dual community in Cambridge has long been known as 'Town and Gown', and life was not always harmonious between the two different factions. Many disturbances and riots took place in medieval times, largely due to resentment caused by privileges granted to the powerful university authorities. Rich college founders and benefactors often purchased much of the land and property, and as the university became more established its powers were gradually increased. The Chancellor of the university, along with the Masters of the colleges, also gained the right in law to try all civil and criminal cases in which a university member was involved. This was officially named the Chancellor's Court but soon became known as The Townsmens' Scourge, as some academics took advantage of the protection it afforded. A particularly bad riot in 1261 resulted in damage to many houses and the burning of university records. When the case was tried, 16 townsmen and 28 scholars were found guilty. The scholars received the King's pardon but the townsmen were all hanged for inciting the riot. During the English Civil Wars of the mid 17th century, conflict once again arose on a serious scale as the townspeople were Parliamentarians, while the academics were predominantly Royalists. The great Parliamentarian leader, Oliver Cromwell, was a native of East Anglia and a graduate of the university, as well as MP for Cambridge from 1640-49. Cromwell raised an army of 30,000 men in 1643 to protect Cambridge against Royalist forces, and later became Lord Protector of the English Commonwealth after the execution of Charles I. Regardless of the upheaval caused in these times of social and political unrest, Town and Gown learnt to live together and the town evolved its own character alongside university and college expansion.

In the early days of the university, students lived in small hostels or halls, though these were soon superseded by colleges founded by kings and queens, leading aristocrats, members of the clergy and others. The first Cambridge college, Peterhouse, was founded in 1284 by Hugh de Balsham, Bishop of Ely and, the most recent, Robinson, in 1977 by Sir David Robinson, a local businessman. There are 31 colleges, some more famous than others owing to their celebrity founders, such as King's College, founded in 1441 by Henry VI as a dual foundation with Eton School, and Trinity College, founded in 1546 by the most famous of English kings, Henry VIII. As the colleges evolved they gradually took over the centre of Cambridge, resulting in the demolition of streets and houses to make way for the visions of their founders, as was the case at both King's and Trinity. Around this time the course of the river Cam was diverted slightly to the east to run closer to the town and take a route through the back gardens of the central colleges, from where the name 'The Backs' derives. This has resulted in the river flowing through beautiful gardens, under bridges and past amazing college buildings, contributing much to the romance of Cambridge, something that Oxford does not have in quite the same way. It is along The Backs in that area anciently known as 'The Thousand Willows', that the famous Cambridge pastime of punting takes place, a great way to glimpse the heart of the city.

The all-important river is, of course, Cambridge's *raison d'être*, from which it takes its name: *bridge* over the river *Cam* - Cam bridge. It is partly what makes the place so special, dividing into three parts as it passes through on its journey to the North Sea: the upper river in the meadows around Grantchester; The Backs which run through the centre; and the lower river towards Fen Ditton where it increases in width and allows competitive rowing to take place, the traditional Oxbridge sport.

The stunning architecture of Cambridge is what everyone comes to see, from the iconic King's College Chapel and the medieval courtyards, through almost all the mainstream architectural styles that are represented here. Many of the great English architects have designed buildings in Cambridge, with three by Sir Christopher Wren, including his first completed structure, Pembroke College Chapel of 1663-65. As well as all the beautiful architecture of the past, there is also an impressive collection of modern buildings. Cambridge is rich in its architectural heritage, made possible by the wealth of the university and, particularly, by the individual colleges who have built consistently over the last eight centuries.

The university in Cambridge is one huge campus intermingled with the other buildings of the town. The colleges, where the students live, have been the temporary homes of an endless list of famous people who have studied here: over a dozen English Prime Ministers; scientists such as Newton, Darwin, Cockroft and Walton, Crick and Watson, and Stephen Hawking; poets and writers including Marlowe, Milton, Wordsworth, Byron, Tennyson, Ted Hughes, Salman Rushdie, Nick Hornby and Zadie Smith; and an array of celebrities across the contemporary media world, many of whom cut their teeth in the famous Cambridge Footlights student theatre. Cambridge has more Nobel prize winners to its credit than any other university, and came top in the world university rankings in 2011~12.

Today, Cambridge leads the international academic community and, as testimony to its modern prowess in such areas as bio-technology, the city is surrounded by science and business parks spawned by the university and given the nickname 'Silicon Fen', where it is home to such important research as the Human Genome Project. Life here continues to be as rich and vibrant as ever, from the serious activities of exams and graduations, to the fun of May Balls and boat races, and the cycle continues and grows year after year in this place of such humble beginnings..........

Tim Rawle, Spring 2012

Classic CAMBRIDGE

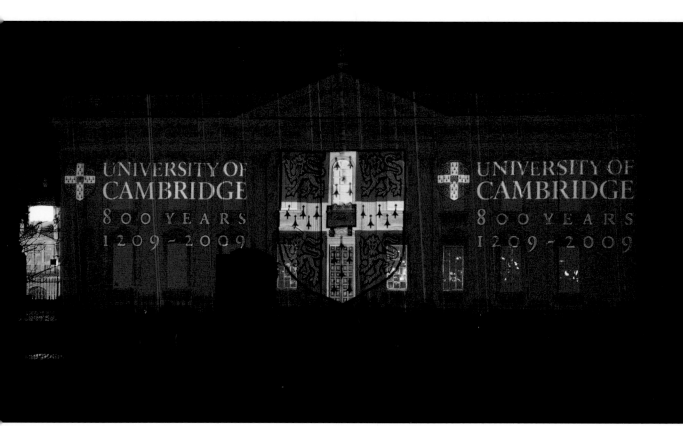

Celebratory projection on the University Senate House

Following pages: Cambridge city centre looking south, with Great Court of Trinity College in the foreground

Left: *King's College Chapel from The Backs*   Above: *King's College with the fields of south Cambridge beyond* 15

King's College Chapel, the west elevation

Right: East end of the nave, King's College Chapel

(Photograph taken with the assistance of James Austin)

17

Angels with trumpets, the Organ, King's College Chapel

The Screen, King's College Chapel, built during the time of Henry VIII and his second queen, Anne Boleyn, 1533-36   19
(Photograph taken with the assistance of James Austin)

Golden Dragon, the West Door, King's College Chapel

King's College Choristers en-route to Chapel

Ready for Dinner ~ The Hall, King's College
(Photograph taken with the assistance of Paul Smith)

King's College Bridge

My heart is sick for several things, only to be found in King's
I do recall those haunts with tears, the Backs, the Chapel and the Rears
O places of perpetual mire, localities of my desire, O lovely, O remembered gloom......
Haunts where I drank the whole damn night! Place where I catted till the light!
Dear spot where I was taken short. O Bodley's Court! O Bodley's Court!

Rupert Brooke, 1913

The Bridge and Bodley's Court, King's College

Above: Frozen Mulberry, Bodley's Court, King's College
Previous pages: Twilight over Cambridge

May Ball Marquee, King's College

King's College from the West ~ cows grazing on Scholars Piece
Right: Winter Painter, King's College Backs

Bikes in Snow, King's College Screen, King's Parade

King's Parade

Left: Henry VIII, King's College   Above: Senior Dons in King's Parade
Following pages: the long back of King's College Chapel from the North

The Evangelist St. John my patron was:
Three Gothic courts are his; and in the first
Was my abiding-place, a nook obscure......

William Wordsworth (1770-1850)

Above: St. John's College Gatehouse from All Saint's Passage   Right: St. John The Evangelist on the Gatehouse
Previous pages: Cambridge from the West

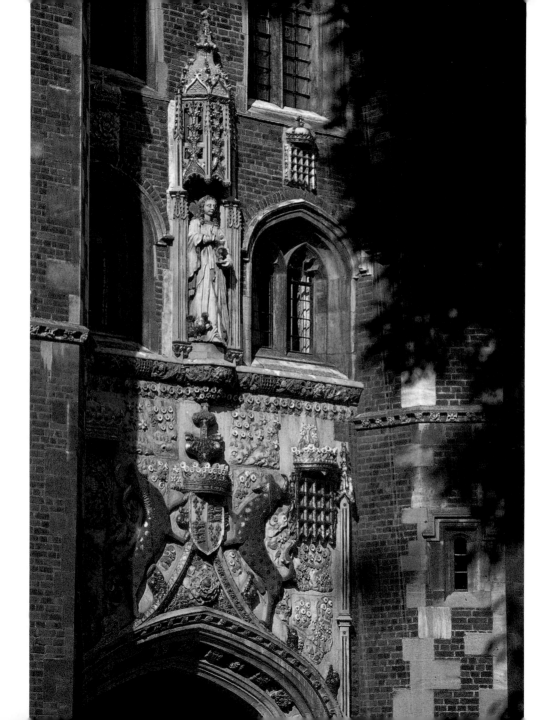

Formal Hall, St. John's College
Right: St. John's Choristers, New Court Cloister

The Bridge of Sighs, St. John's College

The 'Wren' Bridge ~ Above: Old Father Cam watching over the river   Below: Neptune

Chauffeured Punt ~ The 'Wren' Bridge, St. John's College

St. John's College from the West

St. John's College Chapel from Trinity College Backs

Punting through St. John's College
Following pages: New Court and the Bridge of Sighs, St. John's College

Trinity College Gatehouse ~ graduands en-route to The Senate House
Right: The Fountain and Gatehouse, Great Court, Trinity College

Nevile's Gate, Trinity College

Evening Concert, The Old Combination Room, Trinity College
(Photograph taken with the assistance of Paul Smith)

Tennyson and Newton, the antechapel, Trinity College

QUAM IN DIE

...MOARE
...E HODGSON
J H HOLLINS
J W HOPKINS
R HORN
A R P L HORNBY
A J P G HOWARD
R G HOWEY
T HOWITT
T W G HULBERT
C S HUMPHRIES
F W JACKSON
T R E JACKSON
D H JACOBSON
D J S W JARVIE
M J ESB
R E JEFFERY
B J JEFFREYS
E J JESSUP
A JOHNSON
M E G KAUFFMANN
H W KEARNEY
J KEE
D W KENT
R G G KERRISON
J F KINGSCOTE
O C KISCH
C M KNAGGS
VISCOUNT
    KNEBWORTH
H G B KNIGHT
X

W J LAWRENCE
W N LEACH
J T LEACOCK
E D W LEAF
E H J LEIGH-CLARE
J H LEWIS
M G LILLINGSTON
H E J LISTER
J H LITTLE
T D LITTLE
J H LIVERSIDGE
R DE M C LLEWELLYN
W G LUCAS
M LUXMOORE
R J W MCALLEN
R E MACCAW
R M McCOSH
E G MACGREGOR
A R MacINTYRE
W M MACKEAN
W M MACLEAN
A C MAC-PHERSON
A G MAINWARING
ELLERKE.SONSLG...
VISCOUNT
    MAITLAN...
W R MALLORY
W W E MANN
E D H MANSON-BAH...
E M B MARTYN
D P F C MAUCHLE...
C MAURICE ROBER...
J R C METCALFE...

D L MITCHELL
F LEES
N L PISAN...
D W PITMAN
R W PURVITT
J S FOSTER
B LOWELL
R J K ES ON
R M PROCTER
A S PROCTOR
D J RA VSEV...
E...
NOLDS
...DES
...NSON
...KER

R H PINCKNEY
...
...
...
...
...
...
...
...
SIR...ON

R H STEVENS...
B H STEWART
W A B STIRLING
J M STOREY
J G STRANG STEEL
T S STRUTHERS
T S BRUGERS
J STUART
VISCOUNT STUART
J S SWANN
G H SWIFT
J D A SYRETT
C G TANNER
E J TARRANT
J R N TATE
T O TAYLOR
W TAYLOR-YOUNG
C L TENNYSON
J FETTLEY
J D A THARP
A E THICKETT
P M H THOMAS
G S THOMSON
D THOMSSON
D S THOMSON
S THORPE
B K TICHE
P B TOMKIN
J E O REHERNE

H J TUFNELL
W M TURNBULL
J TURNER
J H TYLER
A D T URBAN-EMMRICH
C S VANDERSPAR
E VERNEY
W WAKE
C W WALCOTT
C H WALKER
A C WASHINGTON
M L WATNEY
M H WEAVER
C F WEBSTER
E F WEBSTER
J M WEDDERSPOON
C L E WELLS
N R WHEATCROFT
K L WHITESMITH
L E WIDGERON
C E M WIGGINS
A F WIGRAM
W N WILLIAMSON
    NORSE
SIR G P V WILLS Bt
A G & C WILSON
G N WILSON
J R WILSON
R F WILSON
C WINCH
A G WORMALD
M D WORTHINGTON-
    JONES
P A L WRIGHT
R V WRIGHTSON
M J J YONGE
L R YOUNGER
T ZISSU
B H SYMES

59

The Avenue, Trinity College

The Bridge and Avenue, Trinity College

Winter Punts, Trinity College Backs

Autumn Punts, Trinity College Backs

Above: Queens' College   Right: The Mathematical Bridge, Queens' College
Previous pages: The old front, Queens' College, Queens' Lane

The Master's Lodge, Christ's College
Previous pages: Old Court, Corpus Christi, with the Anglo-Saxon tower of St. Bene't's Church

Quincentenary Procession, Old Court, Christ's College

Above: Red Dragon, The Screens Passage, Christ's College   Right: Keystone Angel, Westminster College
Following pages: The Pepys Building, Magdalene College

The West Range, Downing College
Following pages: The East Range, Downing College

The Hall, Downing College

Above: The Chapel, Peterhouse   Right: Pembroke College Chapel by Sir Christopher Wren
Following pages: Emmanuel College Chapel by Sir Christopher Wren

Off to graduate: Left: Gonville and Caius graduands and the Gate of Honour;   Above: Jesus College graduands **87**
Previous pages: Summer dawn, Cambridge city centre

Above: Romantic Cambridge ~ Old Schools Oriel, Trinity Lane
Left: St. John's College graduands leaving for the Senate House

Clare College Bridge, the oldest bridge over the river Cam ~ 1639-40 by Thomas Grumbold
Previous pages: Clearing the leaves   Following pages: view from the south

Above: Punting through the willows   Right: To Grantchester for tea
Following pages: the central colleges and The Backs

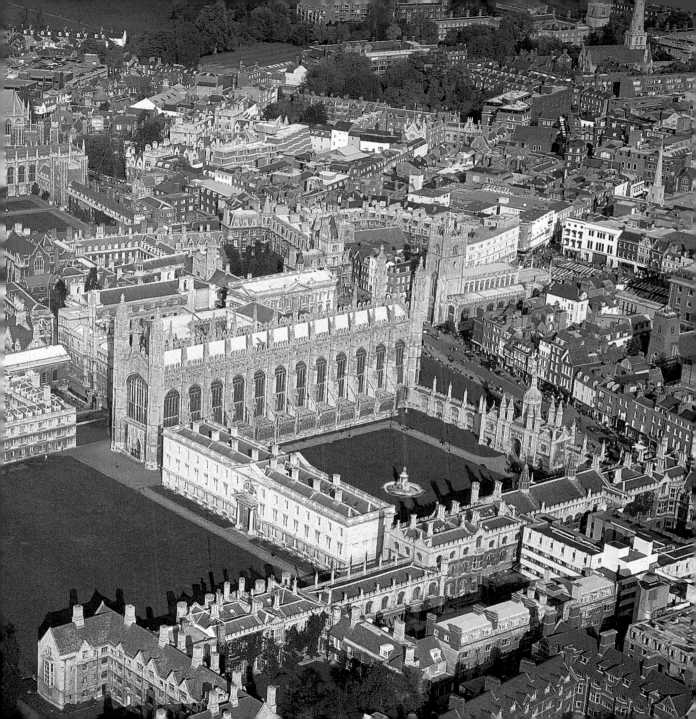

Queuing for the Ball ~ Pembroke

Off to the Ball ~ Trinity Lane

GARDE TA FOY

At The Ball ~ Magdalene & Peterhouse

Playing at The Ball ~ Emmanuel

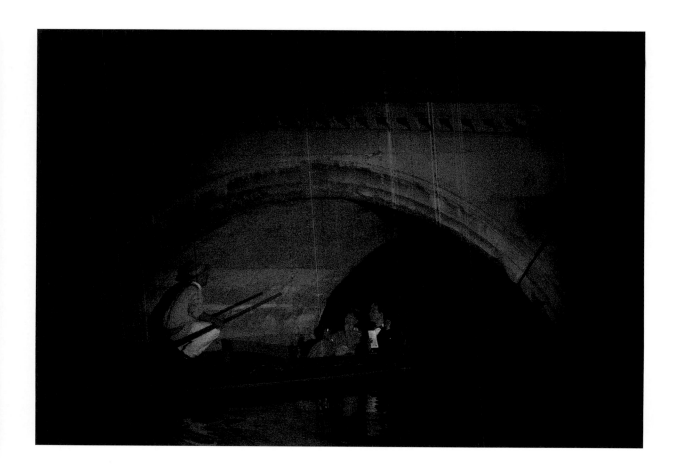

Punting at The Ball ~ Trinity Bridge

Cooling off ~ May Ball 'Survivors' photo, 6 a.m., Trinity College Backs
Right: The morning after ~ Great Court, Trinity, 7 a.m.

The Senior Combination Room, Downing College, by Howell, Killick, Partridge & Amis (1966-70)
Previous Pages: Magdalene Street shops and houses

The Hall, Fitzwilliam College, by Sir Denys Lasdun (1961-67)

The Møller Centre, Churchill College, by Henning Larsen (1992)

The Law Faculty by Foster Associates (1995)

Previous pages: The annual college boat races ~ May Bumps spectators at Ditton Corner
Above: Victorious Magdalene Ladies rowing home   Right: Jesus Ladies rowing to the start

Willow in their hair ~ successful Homerton Ladies

Stylish Craft at The May Bumps

Winter training

Evening scullers

CAMBRIDGE BLADES ~ Rowing blades of the Cambridge Boat Clubs

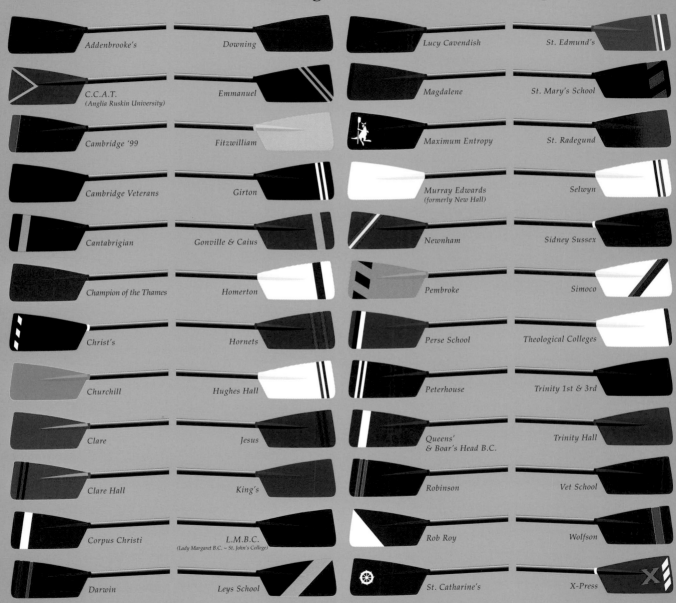

Addenbrooke's

Downing

Lucy Cavendish

St. Edmund's

C.C.A.T.
(Anglia Ruskin University)

Emmanuel

Magdalene

St. Mary's School

Cambridge '99

Fitzwilliam

Maximum Entropy

St. Radegund

Cambridge Veterans

Girton

Murray Edwards
(formerly New Hall)

Selwyn

Cantabrigian

Gonville & Caius

Newnham

Sidney Sussex

Champion of the Thames

Homerton

Pembroke

Simoco

Christ's

Hornets

Perse School

Theological Colleges

Churchill

Hughes Hall

Peterhouse

Trinity 1st & 3rd

Clare

Jesus

Queens'
& Boar's Head B.C.

Trinity Hall

Clare Hall

King's

Robinson

Vet School

Corpus Christi

L.M.B.C.
(Lady Margaret B.C. ~ St. John's College)

Rob Roy

Wolfson

Darwin

Leys School

St. Catharine's

X-Press

Cambridge University

City of Cambridge

Rowing home at The May Bumps ~ The Long Reach, Fen Ditton meadows

......my special thanks to Anita for help putting this book together TR

UNIVERSITY OF
CAMBRIDGE

Classic CAMBRIDGE
University Edition